# This Baby Book: The First 5 Years

## Is Dedicated To:

_____

# DEDICATION

This book is dedicated to all the new parents out there.

You are my inspiration in producing baby books especially to record keepsake memories that will last a lifetime.

# How To Use This Baby Book; The First Five Years Keepsake Log Book:

This ultimate baby book the first five years notebook is a perfect way to track and record all your new baby memories. This unique baby's book: the first 5 years notebook is a great way to keep all of your keepsake information all in one place.

Each interior page includes prompts and space to record the following:

1. Great Expectations - Write the memories of the baby's arrival in the journal notes.

2. Welcome To The World - Record the baby's arrival and important memories of that day. And the first five years as well.

3. Dear Baby - Construct your love letter and the heart feels you'd like to share..upon birth and through the first five years. so as to be reminded later when reminiscing...

4. Baby's First through 5th Year - Record funny, silly and important events about the baby's first through the 5th year.

5. Take a photo, record your thoughts - Stay on task using this photo page to insert your favorite picture of your baby from ages 1 -5. Special memories can be written right on the page.

6. Birthday Page - Space to put a yearly picture of the baby while celebrating the birthday milestones.

7. Monthly Progress Report - Record milestones of baby's first through the 5th year.

8. Note Pages - For more journaling and thoughts on baby's growth. Write out all the heartfelt memories of love for your new baby.

9. Say Cheese - baby's tooth page, so to keep track of when the teething begins.

10. Family Tree - Record on both sides of the family, so the baby can trace family lineage.

Have Fun!

# BABY BOOK
## The first 5 years
### — GREAT EXPECTATIONS —

# BABY BOOK
## The first 5 years
### — GREAT EXPECTATIONS —

_____
_____
_____
_____
_____
_____
_____
_____
_____
_____
_____
_____
_____
_____
_____
_____
_____

# BABY BOOK
## The first 5 years
### — GREAT EXPECTATIONS —

# BABY BOOK
## The first 5 years
— WELCOME TO THE WORLD —

_____
_____
_____
_____
_____
_____
_____
_____
_____
_____
_____
_____
_____

# BABY BOOK
## The first 5 years
— WELCOME TO THE WORLD —

# BABY BOOK
## The first 5 years
### — WELCOME TO THE WORLD —

_____
_____
_____
_____
_____
_____
_____
_____
_____
_____
_____
_____
_____
_____
_____
_____

# BABY BOOK
## The first 5 years
### — DEAR BABY —

# BABY BOOK
## The first 5 years
### — DEAR BABY —

# BABY BOOK
## The first 5 years
### — DEAR BABY —

# BABY BOOK
## The first 5 years
### — ALL ABOUT BABY —

# BABY BOOK
## The first 5 years
### — ALL ABOUT BABY —

# BABY BOOK
## The first 5 years
### — ALL ABOUT BABY —

# BABY BOOK
## The first 5 years
### — BABYS FIRST YEAR —

# BABY BOOK
## The first 5 years
### —BABYS FIRST YEAR—

# BABY BOOK
## The first 5 years
### — SAVE YOUR PHOTOS AND —
### RECORD YOUR THOUGHTS

*From the moment you hear the good news through Baby's fifth birthday party!*

_____

_____

_____

_____

_____

# BABY BOOK
## The first 5 years
### — BIRTHDAY PAGE —

# BABY BOOK
## The first 5 years
### — MONTHLY PROGRESS —

# BABY BOOK
## The first 5 years
### — MONTHLY PROGRESS —

# BABY BOOK
## The first 5 years
### —MONTHLY PROGRESS—

# BABY BOOK
## The first 5 years
### — NOTES —

# BABY BOOK
## The first 5 years
— NOTES —

# BABY BOOK
## The first 5 years
### — NOTES —

# BABY BOOK
## The first 5 years
### — NOTES —

# BABY BOOK
## The first 5 years
### — NOTES —

# BABY BOOK
## The first 5 years
### —ONE TO TWO YEARS OLD—

# BABY BOOK
## The first 5 years
### —ONE TO TWO YEARS OLD—

# BABY BOOK
## The first 5 years
### SAVE YOUR PHOTOS AND RECORD YOUR THOUGHTS

*From the moment you hear the good news through Baby's fifth birthday party!*

_____
_____
_____
_____
_____
_____

# BABY BOOK
## The first 5 years
### — BIRTHDAY PAGE —

# BABY BOOK
## The first 5 years
### —MONTHLY PROGRESS—

# BABY BOOK
## The first 5 years
### — MONTHLY PROGRESS —

# BABY BOOK
## The first 5 years
### —MONTHLY PROGRESS—

# BABY BOOK
## The first 5 years
### — NOTES —

# BABY BOOK
## The first 5 years
— NOTES —

# BABY BOOK
## The first 5 years
### — NOTES —

# BABY BOOK
## The first 5 years
### — NOTES —

# BABY BOOK
## The first 5 years
### — NOTES —

**BABY BOOK**
*The first 5 years*
—TWO TO THREE YEARS OLD—

# BABY BOOK
## The first 5 years
### —TWO TO THREE YEARS OLD—

# BABY BOOK
## The first 5 years
### SAVE YOUR PHOTOS AND RECORD YOUR THOUGHTS

*From the moment you hear the good news through Baby's fifth birthday party!*

# BABY BOOK
## The first 5 years
### —BIRTHDAY PAGE—

# BABY BOOK
## The first 5 years
### — MONTHLY PROGRESS —

# BABY BOOK
## The first 5 years
### —MONTHLY PROGRESS—

# BABY BOOK
## The first 5 years
### —MONTHLY PROGRESS—

# BABY BOOK
## The first 5 years
### — NOTES —

# BABY BOOK
## The first 5 years
— NOTES —

# BABY BOOK
## The first 5 years
### — NOTES —

# BABY BOOK
## The first 5 years
### — NOTES —

# BABY BOOK
## The first 5 years
### — NOTES —

# BABY BOOK
## The first 5 years
### —THREE TO FOUR YEARS OLD—

# BABY BOOK
## The first 5 years
### —THREE TO FOUR YEARS OLD—

# BABY BOOK
## *The first 5 years*

— SAVE YOUR PHOTOS AND —
RECORD YOUR THOUGHTS

*From the moment you hear the good news through Baby's fifth birthday party!*

_____
_____
_____
_____
_____
_____

# BABY BOOK
## The first 5 years
### —BIRTHDAY PAGE—

# BABY BOOK
## The first 5 years
### —MONTHLY PROGRESS—

# BABY BOOK
## The first 5 years
### — MONTHLY PROGRESS —

# BABY BOOK
## The first 5 years
### — MONTHLY PROGRESS —

# BABY BOOK
## The first 5 years
— NOTES —

# BABY BOOK
## The first 5 years
— NOTES —

# BABY BOOK
## The first 5 years
### — NOTES —

# BABY BOOK
## The first 5 years
### — NOTES —

# BABY BOOK
## The first 5 years
### — NOTES —

# BABY BOOK
## The first 5 years
### —FOUR TO FIVE YEARS OLD—

# BABY BOOK
## The first 5 years
### —FOUR TO FIVE YEARS OLD—

# BABY BOOK
## The first 5 years
### SAVE YOUR PHOTOS AND RECORD YOUR THOUGHTS

*From the moment you hear the good news through Baby's fifth birthday party!*

_____

_____

_____

_____

_____

_____

# BABY BOOK
## The first 5 years
### — BIRTHDAY PAGE —

# BABY BOOK
## The first 5 years
### — MONTHLY PROGRESS —

# BABY BOOK
## The first 5 years
### — MONTHLY PROGRESS —

# BABY BOOK
## The first 5 years
### — MONTHLY PROGRESS —

# BABY BOOK
## The first 5 years
### — NOTES —

# BABY BOOK
## The first 5 years
### — NOTES —

# BABY BOOK
## The first 5 years
### — NOTES —

# BABY BOOK
## The first 5 years
### — NOTES —

# BABY BOOK
## The first 5 years
— NOTES —

# BABY BOOK
## The first 5 years
— BEYOND FIVE YEARS OLD —

# BABY BOOK
## The first 5 years
### — BEYOND FIVE YEARS OLD —

# BABY BOOK
## The first 5 years
— BEYOND FIVE YEARS OLD —

# BABY BOOK
## The first 5 years
### — BEYOND FIVE YEARS OLD —

# BABY BOOK
## The first 5 years
### — BEYOND FIVE YEARS OLD —

# BABY BOOK
## The first 5 years
### SAVE YOUR PHOTOS AND RECORD YOUR THOUGHTS

From the moment you hear the good news through Baby's fifth birthday party!

_____
_____
_____
_____
_____
_____

# BABY BOOK
## The first 5 years
### — BIRTHDAY PAGE —

# BABY BOOK
## The first 5 years
### — MONTHLY PROGRESS —

# BABY BOOK
## The first 5 years
### — MONTHLY PROGRESS —

# BABY BOOK
## The first 5 years
### —MONTHLY PROGRESS—

# BABY BOOK
## The first 5 years
### — NOTES —

# BABY BOOK
## The first 5 years
### — NOTES —

# BABY BOOK
## The first 5 years
— NOTES —

# BABY BOOK
## The first 5 years
### — NOTES —

# BABY BOOK
## The first 5 years
— NOTES —

# BABY BOOK
## The first 5 years
### — MILESTONE & ACHIEVEMENTS —

Milestone                                                                      Date

Write about an event...

Skipped...

Tied shoes...

Ask how, why and when questions...

Could recite own street and town...

Could string small beads...

Could catch a ball easily

Baby's other milestones and highlights...

# BABY BOOK
## The first 5 years
### — SPECIAL DAYS —

# BABY BOOK
## The first 5 years
### —OUR GROWING FAMILY—

# BABY BOOK
## The first 5 years
### — NOTES —

# BABY BOOK
## The first 5 years
### —OUR GROWING FAMILY—

# BABY BOOK
## The first 5 years
— NOTES —

# BABY BOOK
## The first 5 years
### — OUR GROWING FAMILY —

# BABY BOOK
## The first 5 years
### — NOTES —

# BABY BOOK
## The first 5 years
### —OUR GROWING FAMILY—

# BABY BOOK
## The first 5 years
### — NOTES —

# BABY BOOK
## The first 5 years
### —OUR GROWING FAMILY—

# BABY BOOK
## The first 5 years
### — FAMILY TREE —

**GREAT-GRANDMOTHER**
Name
Birth date & place

**GREAT-GRANDMOTHER**
Name
Birth date & place

**GREAT-GRANDFATHER**
Name
Birth date & place

**GREAT-GRANDFATHER**
Name
Birth date & place

**GREAT-GRANDMOTHER**
Name
Birth date & place

**GREAT-GRANDMOTHER**
Name
Birth date & place

**GREAT-GRANDFATHER**
Name
Birth date & place

**GREAT-GRANDFATHER**
Name
Birth date & place

**MATERNAL GRANDMOTHER**
Name
Birth date & place

**PATERNAL GRANDMOTHER**
Name
Birth date & place

**MATERNAL GRANDFATHER**
Name
Birth date & place

**PATERNAL GRANDFATHER**
Name
Birth date & place

**MOTHER**
Name
Birth date & place

**FATHER**
Name
Birth date & place

**BABY!**
Name

# BABY BOOK
## The first 5 years
— NOTES —

# BABY BOOK
## The first 5 years
### — SAY CHEESE —

Baby began teething at ........................................................

Baby's first tooth appeared at ...............................................

How Baby fared with teething ...............................................

Teething remedies ...............................................................

**WHEN BABY'S TEETH APPEARED**
(Write dates on tooth images.)

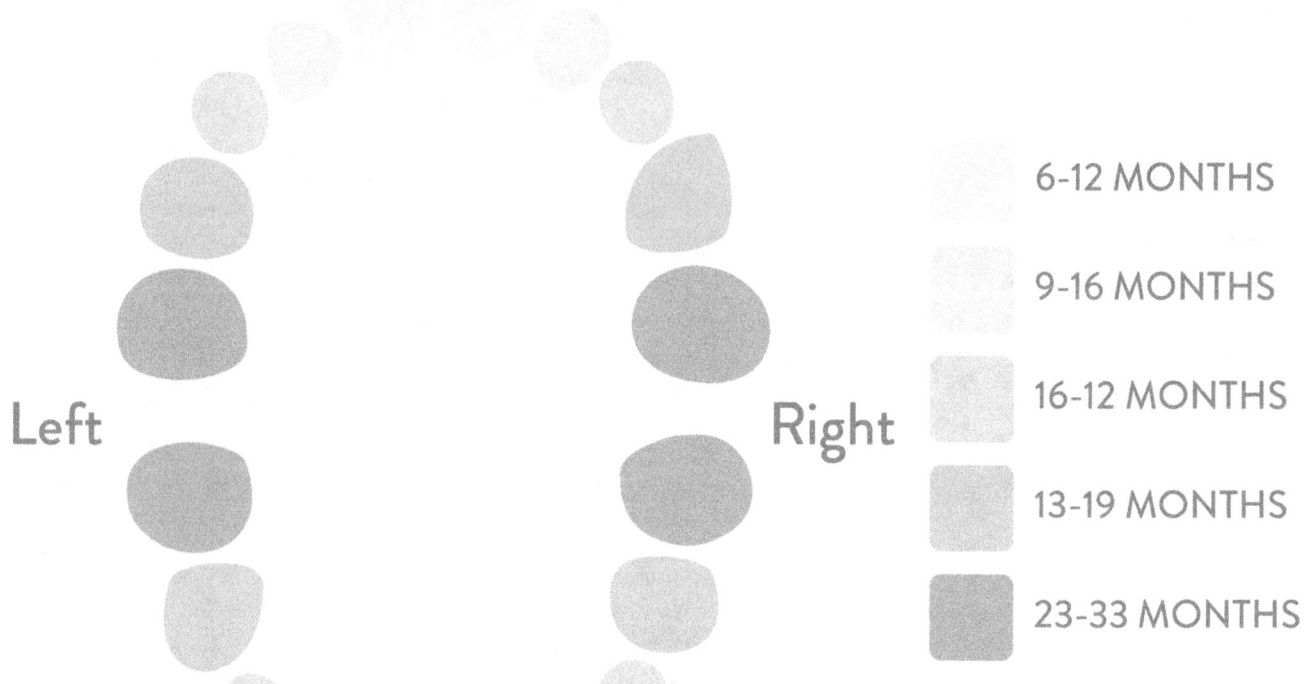

Upper

Left             Right

- 6-12 MONTHS
- 9-16 MONTHS
- 16-12 MONTHS
- 13-19 MONTHS
- 23-33 MONTHS

Lower

# BABY BOOK
## The first 5 years
### — NOTES —

# BABY BOOK
## The first 5 years
— NOTES —

# BABY BOOK
## The first 5 years
### — NOTES —

# BABY BOOK
## The first 5 years
### — NOTES —

# BABY BOOK
## The first 5 years
### — NOTES —

# BABY BOOK
## The first 5 years
### — NOTES —

www.ingramcontent.com/pod-product-compliance
Lightning Source LLC
Chambersburg PA
CBHW081155070526
44583CB00021B/2849